Find It in the
PARK

Dee Phillips

Please visit our web site at: www.garethstevens.com
For a free color catalog describing Gareth Stevens Publishing's list of high-quality books and multimedia programs, call 1-800-542-2595 (USA) or 1-800-387-3178 (Canada). Gareth Stevens Publishing's fax: (414) 332-3567.

Library of Congress Cataloging-in-Publication Data

Phillips, Dee, 1967-
    Find it in the park / by Dee Phillips.
      p. cm. — (Can you find it?)
    ISBN 0-8368-6301-1 (lib. bdg.)
    1. Urban animals—Juvenile literature. 2. Urban plants—Juvenile literature. I. Title.
    QL49.P47   2006
    578.75'5—dc22   2005056347

This North American edition first published in 2006 by
Gareth Stevens Publishing
A Member of the WRC Media Family of Companies
330 West Olive Street, Suite 100
Milwaukee, WI 53212 USA

This U.S. edition copyright © 2006 by Gareth Stevens, Inc. Original edition copyright © 2005 by ticktock Entertainment Ltd. First published in Great Britain in 2005 by ticktock Media Ltd., Unit 2, Orchard Business Centre, North Farm Road, Tunbridge Wells, Kent TN2 3XF.

Gareth Stevens series editor: Dorothy L. Gibbs
Gareth Stevens graphic designer: Charlie Dahl
Gareth Stevens art direction: Tammy West

Picture credits: (t=top, b=bottom, l=left, r=right, c=center)
Alamy: 4-5. FLPA: 3, 4-5, 8b, 10-11b, 15b, 19, 20, 21t, 23.
Every effort has been made to trace the copyright holders for the pictures used in this book. We apologize in advance for any unintentional omissions and would be pleased to insert the appropriate acknowledgements in any subsequent edition.

All rights reserved. No part of this book may be reproduced, stored in a retrieval system, or transmitted in any form or by any means, electronic, mechanical, photocopying, recording, or otherwise, without the prior written permission of the copyright holder.

Printed in the United States of America

1 2 3 4 5 6 7 8 9 10 09 08 07 06

                Words that appear in the glossary are printed in
                boldface type the first time they occur in the text.

Contents

The Park	**4**
Frog	**6**
Water Lily	**8**
Rabbit	**10**
Squirrel	**12**
Snail	**14**
Sunflower	**16**
Honeybee	**18**
Mouse	**20**
Wren	**22**
Glossary	**24**

The Park

There is so much to see in the park, from beautiful flowers and high-flying birds to pond creatures and **scampering** mammals.

What can you find in the park?

Frog

Water lily

Rabbit

Squirrel

Snail

Sunflower

Honeybee

Mouse

Wren

Frog

The kind of frog you are likely to find in a park spends most of its life on land. Its favorite food is insects.

Frogs have long, strong back legs that help them jump very well.

Frogs lay their eggs in ponds or lakes. The eggs of frogs are called spawn.

Frogs and toads look different. Most toads have rough, dry, **warty** skin.

Frogs have smooth, moist skin. Some frogs feel slimy to the touch. Others feel dry.

7

Water Lily

Water lilies are floating flowers with flat, green, heart-shaped leaves. They grow in **freshwater**.

The roots of water lilies grow in the mud at the bottom of a lake or a pond.

The plant grows upward until it reaches the surface of the water.

Water lilies bloom in many beautiful colors, from white or yellow to bright pink.

Rabbit

Rabbits can be found in gardens, fields, and meadows, as well as in parks.

Rabbits hide in their **burrows** most of the day. They usually come out to eat during the night.

Except when rabbits are looking after their young, they are usually alone.

Rabbits eat grass and other plants. They especially like to eat garden vegetables, such as peas, green beans, and lettuce.

Squirrel

There are many different kinds of squirrels in the world. Gray squirrels are the kind most often seen in parks.

Squirrels eat nuts, fruits, flowers, and plant buds.

Squirrels often steal the nuts and seeds that people put out in **feeders** for the birds.

A squirrel's big, bushy tail helps it balance. Squirrels also use their tails to **communicate** with other squirrels.

Snail

A snail has a hard, **spiral** shell to **protect** its soft body. When the snail is frightened, it hides inside its shell.

A snail's head has two pairs of **tentacles**.

A snail moves on only one large, flat foot. Its foot **ripples** as the snail slides along the ground.

Snails leave trails of a slimy **fluid** called **mucus**.

Sunflower

Whether you find them in the park or grow them in a garden, sunflowers are fun flowers.

There are many different varieties of sunflowers. Some kinds grow taller than a person.

Sunflowers have large, bright yellow heads. They turn their heads in the **direction** of the sun.

You may see sunflowers growing in fields. They are used to make sunflower oil for cooking, and sunflower seeds are good to eat.

Honeybee

Honeybees are often found buzzing around parks, especially where there are lots of flowers. Honeybees use **nectar** from flowers to make honey.

In winter, when there are no flowers, bees eat honey from their hives. The honey is stored in specially built **cells** known as honeycomb.

A hive has a queen bee, some **drones**, and lots of workers. The workers collect nectar from flowers.

Mouse

If you find a mouse in the park, it is probably a harvest mouse, which many people call a field mouse. There are many different kinds of mice, and mice are also related to rats.

Most mice have gray or brown fur; large, round ears; and long, thin tails.

When mice get into houses, they can do a lot of **damage**. They can even **gnaw** holes in wood.

Harvest mice make nests in tall grass, and seeds are their favorite food.

21

Wren

More than sixty kinds of birds are known as wrens. Many wrens are small birds that are only about 5 inches (13 centimeters) long.

Some kinds of wrens build their nests in holes inside buildings. Others build nests in trees or among plants such as reeds, or even under rocks.

Most wrens sing a beautiful song, but they can also make loud, chattering noises.

Glossary

burrows – holes that rabbits and other animals dig in the ground to live in

cells – small sections or divisions within a larger space

communicate – to pass on information by talking or making movements that others will understand

damage – harm or injury

direction – the position of something or the way that something is pointing

drones – male bees

feeders – special containers that people fill with food for animals, especially birds

fluid – a liquid, like water, that flows and does not have any certain shape

freshwater – the water in most lakes, rivers, and ponds, which is not salty like seawater

gnaw – to chew, often using long, sharp front teeth

mucus – a slimy coating that protects the skin of some animals and keeps them from drying out

nectar – the sweet liquid found in flowers

protect – to keep safe from harm

ripples – moves with a wavelike motion

scampering – running here and there in short bursts

spiral – curled around in overlapping circles

tentacles – sensitive growths that stick out on an animal's head and are used to feel things

warty – full of bumps that look like warts